A Good Catch

Managing fisheries to meet the nation's demand for seafood

A Good Catch

Managing fisheries to meet the nation's demand for seafood

NOAA FISHERIES SERVICE

written and illustrated by Taylor Morrison

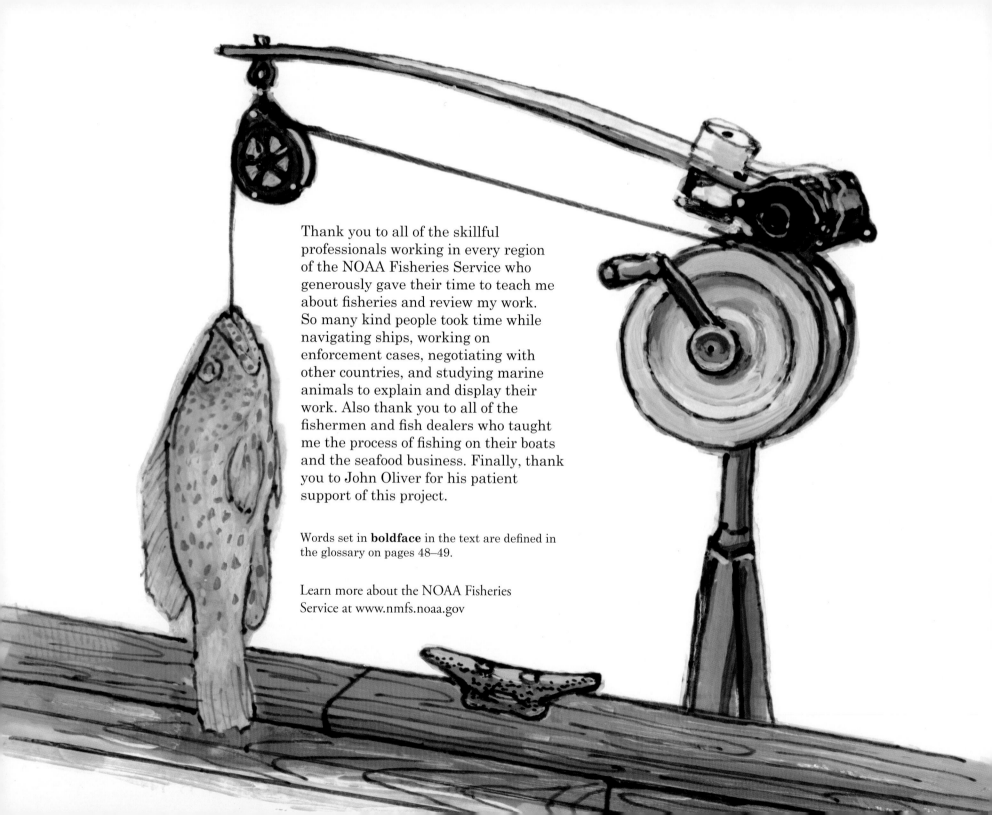

Thank you to all of the skillful professionals working in every region of the NOAA Fisheries Service who generously gave their time to teach me about fisheries and review my work. So many kind people took time while navigating ships, working on enforcement cases, negotiating with other countries, and studying marine animals to explain and display their work. Also thank you to all of the fishermen and fish dealers who taught me the process of fishing on their boats and the seafood business. Finally, thank you to John Oliver for his patient support of this project.

Words set in **boldface** in the text are defined in the glossary on pages 48–49.

Learn more about the NOAA Fisheries Service at www.nmfs.noaa.gov

Contents

6

Sportfishing

From Hawaii up to Alaska, down to California and Texas, and back up to Maine, people love to go saltwater sportfishing. Along America's varied coastline, they enjoy the fresh sea air, seeing pelicans flying over the boat and watching whales breaching nearby.

Sport fishermen use rods and reels that range in size and strength: small ones for five-pound black rockfish, medium ones for twenty-pound mahi-mahi, heavy ones attached to **body harnesses** and fighting chairs to haul in blue marlins or thousand-pound bluefin tuna.

Experienced fishermen know where to find fish in certain parts of the oceans and during specific **fishing seasons**. They know which fish hide under aquatic plants, near **buoys**, and around old abandoned oil rigs. Some fishermen catch fish for food. Others catch and release them using special tools to try to ensure the survival of the fish.

A boy on a charter caught a fish the day after it went out of season. The captain unhooked and tossed the fish back. The boy watched his golden brown prize go *ker-plunk*! into the water and swim away. "It's just one fish. Why can't I keep it? It won't make a difference!" he said in frustration.

Out on the vast ocean it may seem okay to keep all the fish you catch, but fish are a limited resource. Though **anglers** often get angry when they're told how much fish they are allowed to keep, **catch limits** are set to help fish populations rebuild their numbers.

The National Oceanic and Atmospheric Administration (NOAA) Fisheries Service sets these limits to guarantee that sportfishing can continue to generate money and jobs for coastal communities. Setting catch limits also helps protect fish populations and legally protected **species**.

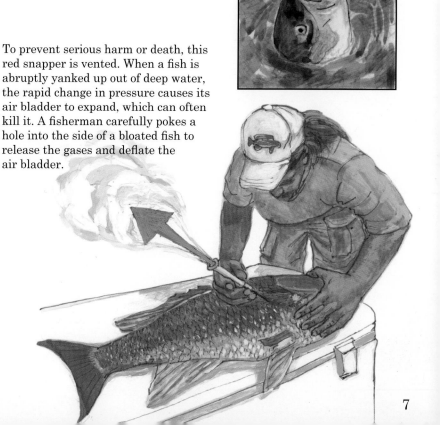

A dehooker can remove hooks and minimize injury to the fish. A fisherman places the rounded end of the tool around the fishing line. Next it is pushed down under the hook inside the fish. Then a quick thrust knocks the fish off the hook and into the water.

To prevent serious harm or death, this red snapper is vented. When a fish is abruptly yanked up out of deep water, the rapid change in pressure causes its air bladder to expand, which can often kill it. A fisherman carefully pokes a hole into the side of a bloated fish to release the gases and deflate the air bladder.

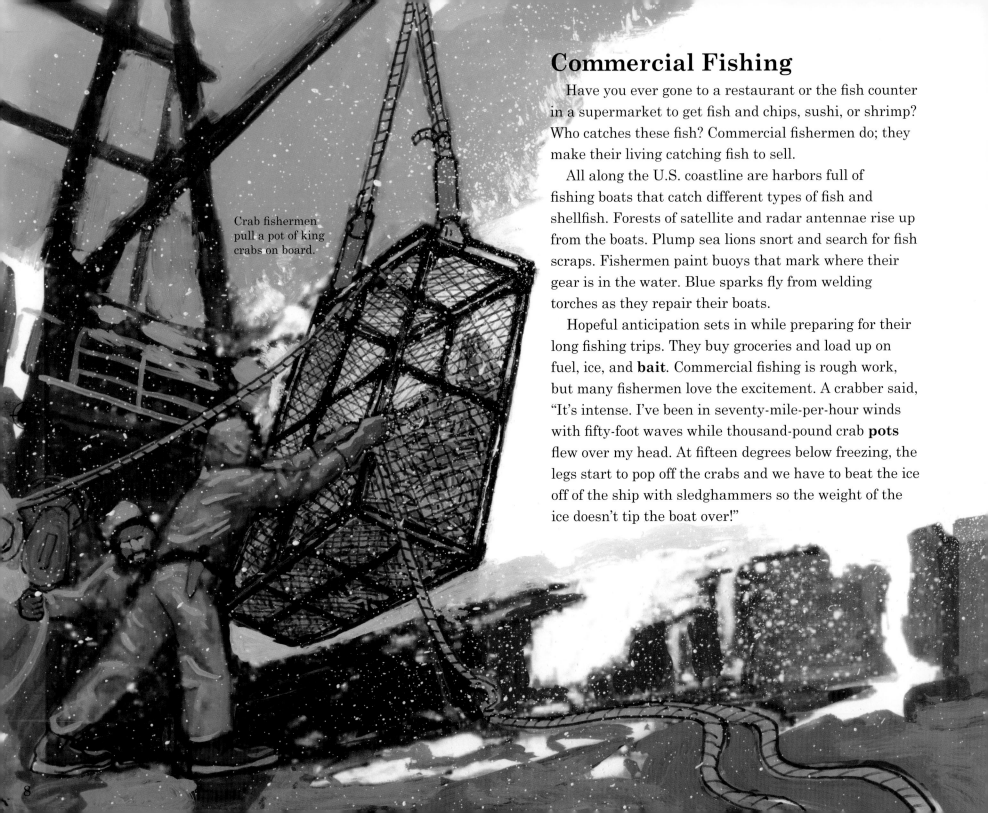

Crab fishermen pull a pot of king crabs on board.

Commercial Fishing

Have you ever gone to a restaurant or the fish counter in a supermarket to get fish and chips, sushi, or shrimp? Who catches these fish? Commercial fishermen do; they make their living catching fish to sell.

All along the U.S. coastline are harbors full of fishing boats that catch different types of fish and shellfish. Forests of satellite and radar antennae rise up from the boats. Plump sea lions snort and search for fish scraps. Fishermen paint buoys that mark where their gear is in the water. Blue sparks fly from welding torches as they repair their boats.

Hopeful anticipation sets in while preparing for their long fishing trips. They buy groceries and load up on fuel, ice, and **bait**. Commercial fishing is rough work, but many fishermen love the excitement. A crabber said, "It's intense. I've been in seventy-mile-per-hour winds with fifty-foot waves while thousand-pound crab **pots** flew over my head. At fifteen degrees below freezing, the legs start to pop off the crabs and we have to beat the ice off of the ship with sledghammers so the weight of the ice doesn't tip the boat over!"

Commercial fishermen generally harvest marine life in three ways: with pots, nets, and fishing lines. Steel cages called pots sit on the seafloor and are baited with fish to catch crabs and lobsters. Giant nets called **purse seines** and **trawls** are towed behind ships to **corral** huge numbers of herring, salmon, and pollock. A 500-foot-long trawl can fill up with 300,000 pounds of fish. **Gill nets** and **longlines** are released into the water with anchors and buoys. The nets and lines are set for many hours until the catches are retrieved. Names of fishing gear describe where they are used. Bottom longlines sit on the seafloor catching flatfish like halibut and sole. **Pelagic** longlines, which are used above the bottom, catch fish like tuna and swordfish.

Working in longlining can be dangerous: Hooks can snag a person's eyes. One fisherman quit after he watched a hook carry away his finger. A Florida longliner laughed when he lifted up his shirt to show a large scar where a hook tore across his stomach. He said that you should always carry a sharp knife to cut the line in case you get tangled up in it.

Two longline fishermen clip baited hooks onto the main line.

Types of commercial fishing vessels and their gear

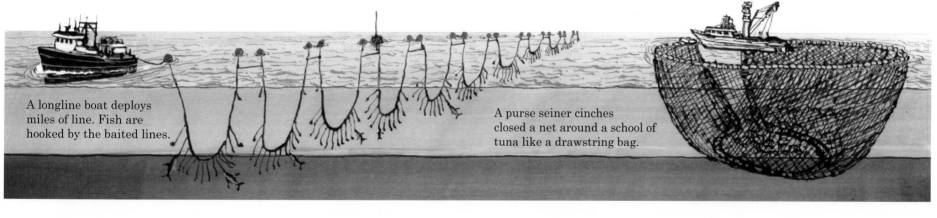

A longline boat deploys miles of line. Fish are hooked by the baited lines.

A purse seiner cinches closed a net around a school of tuna like a drawstring bag.

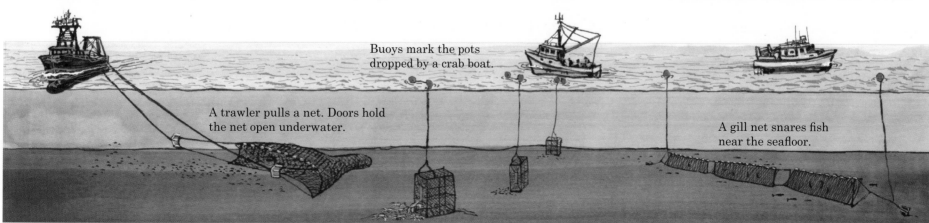

Buoys mark the pots dropped by a crab boat.

A trawler pulls a net. Doors hold the net open underwater.

A gill net snares fish near the seafloor.

Fish Processing

When commercial fishing vessels return to port, they unload their catch. The fish are then processed and packaged for sale. Fish-processing operations range from a single person at the dock filleting a few dozen fish, to enormous processing plants like those in the port of Dutch Harbor, Alaska, that can handle more than 600 million pounds of fish and crabs a year. Here cranes lift giant baskets of wriggling crabs off of crab boats. Big tubes vacuum fish out of the trawlers docked in front of the factories. Squawking ravens and eagles pick fish scraps off of the enormous nets wrapped up on the boats. Big factory trawlers catch and package fish out at sea. The boats are full of workers and machines that **fillet** fish or turn it into a protein paste called surimi used to make imitation crabmeat. When the catcher-processor boats get to shore, workers unload thousands of boxes from the freezing cold fish **holds**. Tons of frozen pollock and cod are shipped to schools, hospitals, and the military.

More than 4,000 miles south of Dutch Harbor is another major fish-processing operation. Longline boats docked in Honolulu, Hawaii, unload tens of thousands of pounds of fish in the morning darkness. The big fish are carted to a huge, cold warehouse. There, a noisy fish auction takes place at five A.M. every day. Standing in front of tuna and swordfish, the auctioneer yells prices per pound until a wholesaler buys it. "One dollar! Ninety cents! Eighty cents! Next one!" The auction starts early so the wholesalers have time to buy and sell the fish in the same day. Then they ship the high-quality fish to restaurants and seafood dealers all over the world.

Fishing supports big enterprises, but it also supports many small businesses. In fishing towns like Cortez, Florida, and Gloucester, Massachusetts, fishermen still fish for a living despite the difficulties because they love the work and want to continue the family tradition. A fisherman from Kodiak, Alaska, said, "I told my mom I was going to work on a fishing boat for the summer and never came back. That was forty years ago."

A factory trawler unloads in Dutch Harbor, Alaska.

At the fish auction in Honolulu, Hawaii, the fish are cut to show that their meat is fresh.

Fish Farming

Fish and shellfish farming or aquaculture has become one of the fastest-growing forms of food production in the world. Aquaculture helps meet the increasing demand for seafood on dinner tables in the United States and abroad. Experts predict that the seafood supply from aquaculture will soon surpass the supply of wild fish and shellfish. Some fish are raised on farms and sold for human food or fertilizer, others are released into the wild to increase their numbers. White sea bass and the eastern oyster are two species that scientists are trying to restore through aquaculture.

Farm-raised freshwater or ocean fish grow in a very different environment than wild fish. Everything about the farmed fish's world is controlled. The water temperature and lighting are altered to convince adults it is **spawning** season so that they release eggs and sperm into the water. The water conditions and feeding cycles are also carefully monitored to ensure the fragile baby fish, known as larval fish, will survive. It takes a lot of skill to be a successful seafood farmer.

Most of the seafood farmed in America is shellfish. Oysters, clams, mussels and a geoduck, which looks like a cross between a clam and a giant worm, are raised with different equipment than fish. Underneath big mussel rafts, mussel seeds grow out of tube socks and attach onto ropes. Once they are mature, tens of thousands of mussels can be harvested from a single raft.

1. Adult white sea bass, yellowtail, halibut, and other fish spawn in tanks.

2. **Fertilized** eggs are caught in bins called egg catchers.

3. Newborn fish hatch from eggs in incubation tanks.

4. Tiny **crustaceans** and **algae** are grown in tanks on-site to feed the larval fish.

Aquaculture is necessary and controversial. Some people are worried about how seafood farming affects the environment; others are working hard to make sure it doesn't.

An aquaculturist from Maine expressed this view, "Thousands of years ago, people domesticated wild fowl for food. Chickens and turkeys bred on farms don't look anything like their wild ancestors. Today, people are in the early stages of domesticating fish, because there is not enough fish in the oceans to feed the growing number of people on Earth."

5. Many farmers use a robot like this one to drop food pellets into tanks to feed the growing fish.

6. Some fish are moved to larger tanks as they grow to market size. At some farms, the growing fish are put into floating pens near shore or out in the open sea.

Managing Fisheries

Bigger, faster boats, improved fishing gear, and navigational tools have enabled the fishing industry to meet the growing need for fish. Global Positioning System (GPS) satellite navigation can guide boats to the exact locations where the fish are. But there is a danger that too many fish will be taken out of the ocean too quickly. The NOAA Fisheries Service works with the fishing industry to ensure that there will be enough fish for future generations.

NOAA scientists first have to determine the size of **fish stocks**. But how can they count fish when fish are hard to see most of the time and constantly moving? It's impossible to count every single fish in the ocean, so **fishery** biologists estimate. They gather as much information as possible about fish stocks, including ages, sizes, abundance, breeding habits, food sources, **predators**, habitats, and migration patterns to ensure accurate estimates.

The NOAA Fisheries Service also gets information by maintaining catch histories from fishing boats. It employs port agents at the docks and observers on fishing boats to record fishermen's catches. They collect information that is called fishery-dependent data. The agents and observers jot down the physical characteristics of the fish and note if any of the wrong species has been caught. Some fishermen don't mind observers, and others hate to be watched all of the time. One observer in Alaska said the fishermen looked after her like a bunch of protective dads.

The work can be dangerous. An observer on a longline boat from Hawaii turned to see a forty-foot wall of green water crashing over him. He said it felt like being in a washing machine as the wave tossed him overboard across the sharp fishing hooks on the deck. He thought he was going to drown and desperately reached up for one last gasp of air when the captain grabbed him and saved his life. Despite the dangers, the data collected by the agents and observers are essential to successfully manage fish populations.

The NOAA Ship *Pisces*
ready for launch in
Moss Point, Mississippi

NOAA's Fleet

In addition to monitoring commercial fishing boats, the NOAA Fisheries Service uses ships to conduct research and survey the oceans. The information they collect is called fishery-independent data. Both men and women work as NOAA Corps officers, licensed engineers, professional fishermen, and other mariners such as cooks. The crews spend a lot of time at sea; they work twelve-hour shifts about 245 days a year. The officers must be very skilled navigators because some areas they survey are remote and dangerous. The ship's captain keeps a close eye on the **echo sounder**, which shows the depth and terrain of the ocean floor passing beneath the ship. "We watch it very closely for pinnacle rocks," said one captain while passing through Alaska's Aleutian Islands. Powerful storms can rock the boats so much that people have to drop to the ground and crawl to avoid being flung around. Sometimes big waves slam into the side of the ships–*BOOM!*–sounding like a giant sledgehammer hitting the **hull**. During really rough weather, the crew members have to hold on to the bars on their bunk beds to keep from bouncing out.

NOAA Corp officers on the bridge of the *Oscar Dyson*. NOAA Corp officers support NOAA's missions by operating nineteen ships and twelve aircraft. In 1999, Evelyn Fields became the first woman to head the NOAA Corps.

A NOAA vessel runs an acoustic survey.

Centerboard

Krill

Fish

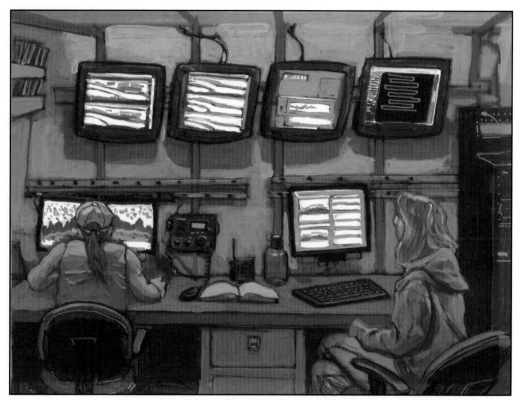

Two scientists working in the acoustic laboratory

NOAA's ships find fish the same way whales and dolphins do: They transmit and receive a wide range of sound waves. An instrument called an echo sounder sends out pulses of sound through the ship's centerboard, a ten-ton fin that extends below the **keel**. The sound waves bounce off fish, plankton, and the seafloor. When the echoes return to the ship, the sound is turned into pictures called echograms. Inside the ship's acoustic laboratory, a room nicknamed the "cave," scientists looking at computer screens see fuzzy blue clouds of krill and giant red blobs indicating schools of fish. The acoustic surveys help the NOAA Fisheries Service estimate how many fish are in an area. Off the coast of Massachusetts, they can observe ten-mile-long schools of herring. NOAA's newer ships like the *Oscar Dyson* were specially designed with sound-damping tiles built into their hulls to muffle the noise of the engines. Scientists want to observe the natural behavior of fish, so they try to stay quiet to avoid disturbing the fish.

Sample Catches

NOAA's fleet of ships catch fish from the oceans bordering the United States. The *Henry B. Bigelow* conducts surveys on the East Coast, and the *Oscar Dyson* does the same on the West Coast.

Scientists catch samples of fish to determine their size, age, and how many males and females there are. They use a variety of gear such as baited pots, longlines, dredges, and trawls. A trawl is unwound on the back deck of the ship. Depending on the location and season, fishermen can be blasted by snow flurries and splashed by giant waves. On the bridge, scientists tell the fishermen how deep to set the net. After a while, the cables pull the full net up out of the foamy water. The fishermen open the back end of the net, and the fish fall out into a bin for the scientists to examine in the onboard laboratory called the wet lab. Scientists measure, weigh, study body parts, and identify species. It is tricky holding on to heavy, slippery, wiggling fish while the boat rocks.

Scientists are particularly interested in monitoring fish by age groups. One of NOAA's main goals is to be sure that enough young fish are left in the ocean to grow up and reproduce. That keeps the fish stock healthy for future generations. Scientists measure a fish's age by counting rings that grow in its scales, **vertebrae**, and ear bones called **otoliths**. It's a lot like counting growth rings on a tree stump.

The back end of the trawl, called the codend, is full of fish.

The crew of the *Oscar Dyson* unwinds a trawl into the water.

A conveyor belt carries fish into the wet lab.

A scientist counts otolith rings under a microscope.

Otolith rings in a vermilion snapper

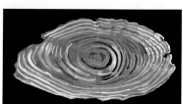

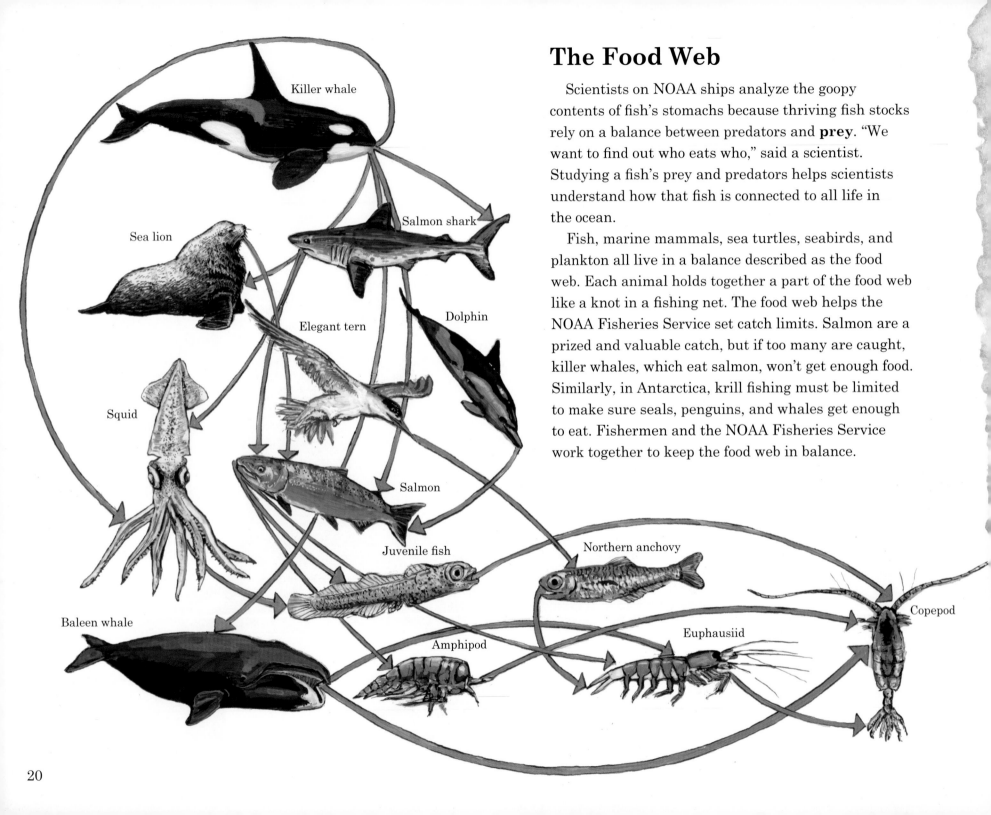

The Food Web

Scientists on NOAA ships analyze the goopy contents of fish's stomachs because thriving fish stocks rely on a balance between predators and **prey**. "We want to find out who eats who," said a scientist. Studying a fish's prey and predators helps scientists understand how that fish is connected to all life in the ocean.

Fish, marine mammals, sea turtles, seabirds, and plankton all live in a balance described as the food web. Each animal holds together a part of the food web like a knot in a fishing net. The food web helps the NOAA Fisheries Service set catch limits. Salmon are a prized and valuable catch, but if too many are caught, killer whales, which eat salmon, won't get enough food. Similarly, in Antarctica, krill fishing must be limited to make sure seals, penguins, and whales get enough to eat. Fishermen and the NOAA Fisheries Service work together to keep the food web in balance.

Killer whale

Salmon shark

Sea lion

Elegant tern

Dolphin

Squid

Salmon

Juvenile fish

Northern anchovy

Copepod

Baleen whale

Amphipod

Euphausiid

Deckhands keep watch on a trawl as it is reeled in.

A water-monitoring device on a metal frame, called a CTD, is lowered from a NOAA ship. It measures the conductivity and temperature of the water at various depths.

22

Phytoplankton

At the base of the food web are floating microscopic plants called **phytoplankton** that feed everything from huge whales to the tiniest fish. If you weighed all of the phytoplankton in the ocean, they would weigh more than all of the trees and plants on Earth! Phytoplankton grow as deep as sunlight can penetrate seawater, from the surface to about 600 feet down. But most of the oxygen and **nutrients** phytoplankton also need to grow are stored in dark, cold water too deep for sunlight to reach. There is a boundary in the ocean that sharply separates cold, deep waters from warm, sunlit surface waters called a **thermocline**. Phytoplankton can flourish when winds, storms, changing seasons, **upwelling**, and **gyres** break the thermocline and force nutrients locked in the deep waters up to mix into the surface waters.

Scientists plunge instruments called CTDs hundreds to thousands of feet down to collect water samples at different depths and study water characteristics. The water samples enable scientists to better study phytoplankton populations. Scientists constantly monitor water conditions over thousands of miles of ocean because temperature or chemical changes affect all marine life.

1. Twenty-five miles off of the Pacific coast, a scientist scoops up a bucket of seawater.

2. Then she squeezes the seawater through a filter into a beaker.

3. She explains that the green smudge on the filter is phytoplankton.

4. Here are green phytoplankton called diatoms viewed under a microscope.

1. A strong thermocline

2. A broken thermocline

3. Currents running along the equator cause cold, deep waters to rise or upwell into spinning swirls called gyres that break the thermocline.

4. Upwelling also occurs along coasts on the east side of ocean basins. Winds and the earth's rotation push surface waters off the coast, so cold, deep waters rise into their place.

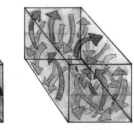

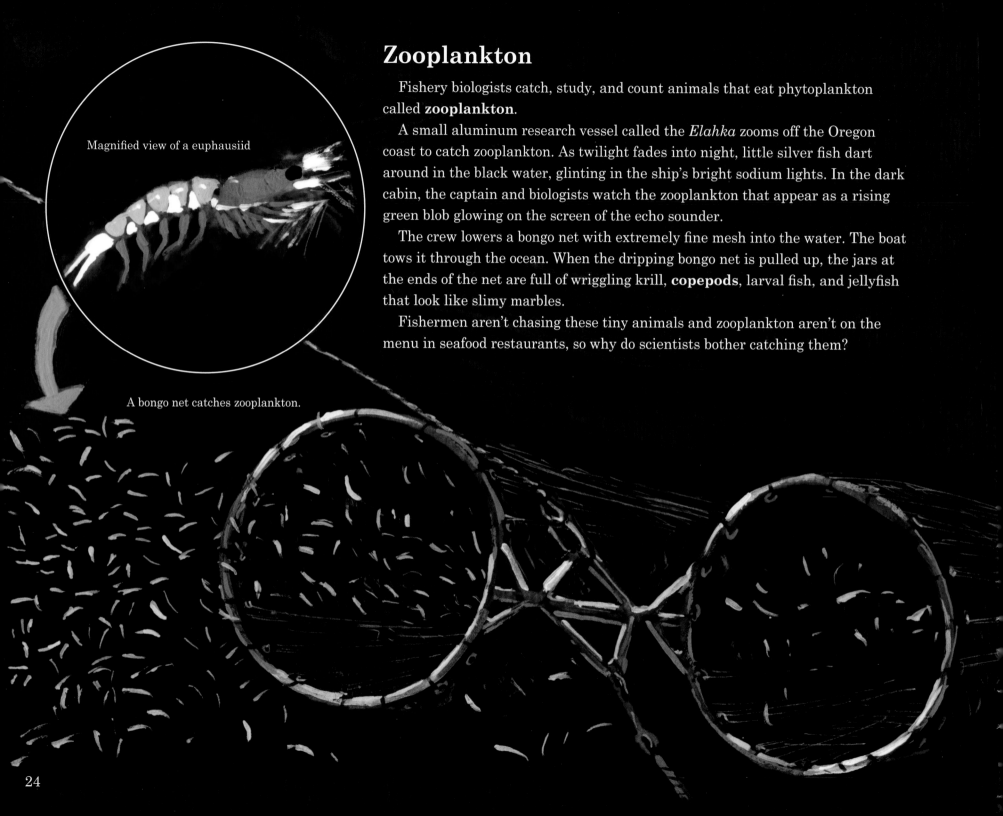

Magnified view of a euphausiid

A bongo net catches zooplankton.

Zooplankton

Fishery biologists catch, study, and count animals that eat phytoplankton called **zooplankton**.

A small aluminum research vessel called the *Elahka* zooms off the Oregon coast to catch zooplankton. As twilight fades into night, little silver fish dart around in the black water, glinting in the ship's bright sodium lights. In the dark cabin, the captain and biologists watch the zooplankton that appear as a rising green blob glowing on the screen of the echo sounder.

The crew lowers a bongo net with extremely fine mesh into the water. The boat tows it through the ocean. When the dripping bongo net is pulled up, the jars at the ends of the net are full of wriggling krill, **copepods**, larval fish, and jellyfish that look like slimy marbles.

Fishermen aren't chasing these tiny animals and zooplankton aren't on the menu in seafood restaurants, so why do scientists bother catching them?

The ship's captain and a scientist watch the echo sounder.

The *Elahka* tows a bongo net.

Zooplankton such as copepods, **amphipods**, and **euphausiids** are a valuable food source for fish, whales, seabirds, and many other animals. The scientists record the quantity and species of zooplankton from each of their catches and use those measurements to estimate the amount of food available for fish to eat. Catch limits are lowered for the kinds of fish they estimate will not have enough to eat.

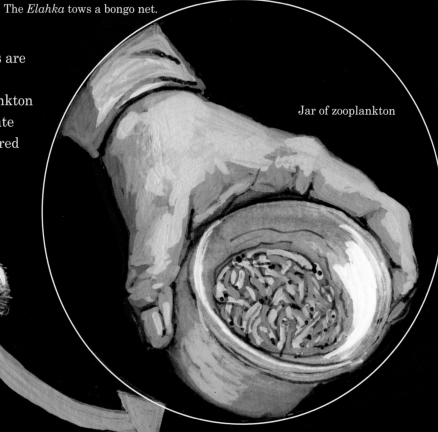

Jar of zooplankton

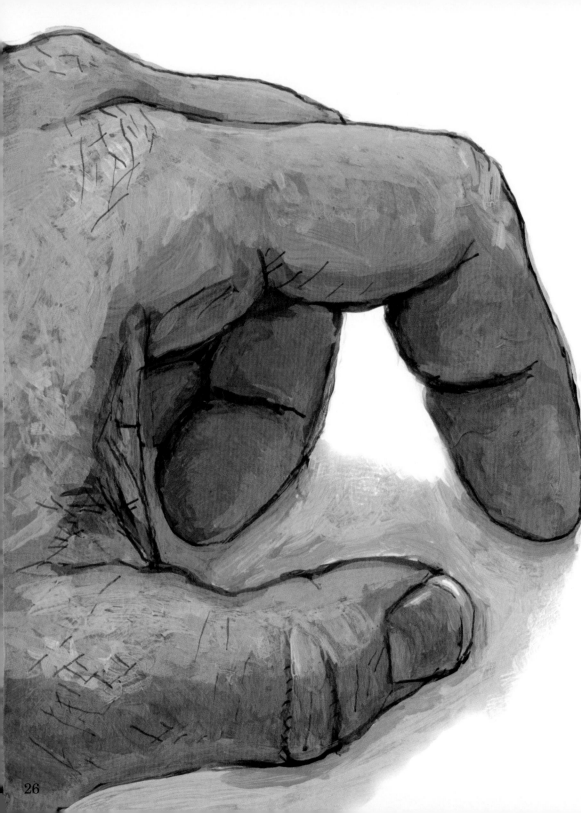

Larval Fish

Zooplankton feed newborn fish called larval fish. After fish eggs hatch, the larval fish float around and eat in masses of tiny animals and plants called plankton. NOAA biologists catch, identify, and record the types and abundance of larval fish and eggs to help them predict how many adult fish there will be. Scientists also learn how ocean temperatures and currents affect the survival of larval fish.

Life is dangerous for larval fish; they are at the mercy of the ocean. A big storm may wash larval fish that are weak swimmers to a place where there is no food or where the water temperature is too hot or too cold. Larval fish must eat a lot and grow fast before something bigger eats them.

Actual size of larval fish

It is difficult to identify larval fish under a microscope because they are so small and do not resemble the adult fish they become. Flatfish such as flounder, halibut, and sole go through an amazing transformation during their first weeks of life. After birth, their eyes are on opposite sides of their heads like most fish. As they mature, one eye moves over their head next to the other eye, and the side with both eyes becomes the top of their body. Some species like the tongue fish (which are shaped like tongues) have an eye that migrates through their head!

The growth stages of a tuna:

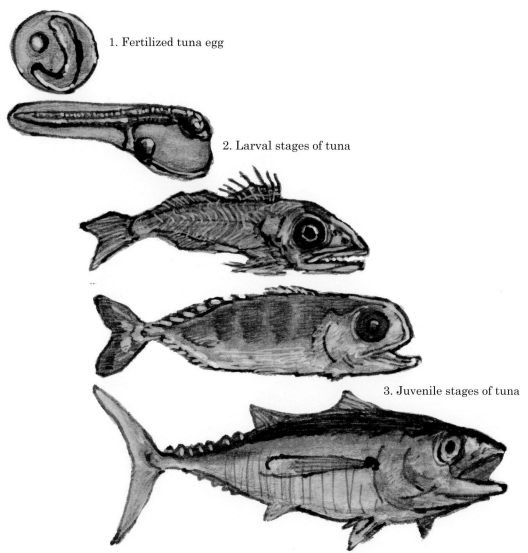

1. Fertilized tuna egg

2. Larval stages of tuna

3. Juvenile stages of tuna

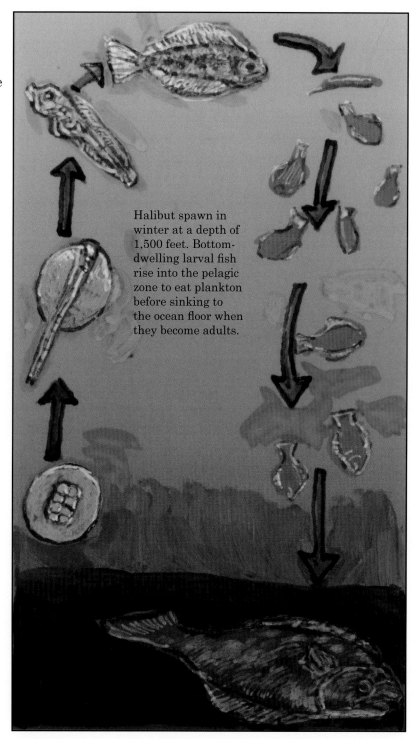

Halibut spawn in winter at a depth of 1,500 feet. Bottom-dwelling larval fish rise into the pelagic zone to eat plankton before sinking to the ocean floor when they become adults.

Marine Ecosystems

Phytoplankton, zooplankton, larval fish, adult fish, and marine mammals all depend on the complex ecosystems in which they live. An **ecosystem** is a community of animals and plants interacting with the land, water, weather, and the surrounding human activities. Marine ecosystems resemble neighborhoods where truck drivers, grocery store owners, teachers, doctors, and many other people each perform a vital function for everyone in the neighborhood. If you remove a certain group, everyone else living there would suffer. Within ecosystems are habitats where fish eat, find shelter, and reproduce. The tropical ocean, tidal wetlands, mangrove swamps, and cold arctic waters are a few marine habitats.

In the Puget Sound area of Washington State, shellfish farmers depend on clean water to grow their oysters, clams, and mussels. But fertilizers and septic waste washing into nearby waterways from roads, yards, and parking lots sometimes harm their crops. Here, a healthy oyster crop is scooped up out of the mud into sorting baskets to be transplanted.

Mangroves and salt marshes provide valuable nursery habitat and shelter for fish. On many coastlines, tropical mangrove swamps and salt marshes have been removed to build condos, marinas, and hotels.

The NOAA Fisheries Service must find out what fish need in their habitats to survive and protect them from harm. Most of the U.S. population lives in coastal areas. The **runoff** of septic waste and fertilizers from those homes, factories, and farms overloads coastal waters with nutrients, which often causes too much phytoplankton to grow. An overgrowth of some kinds of phytoplankton results in poor water quality for fish because it reduces the amount of oxygen in the water.

A less understood threat to marine life comes from carbon dioxide released into the air by cars, planes, and factories. The ocean absorbs the carbon dioxide, and the more it absorbs, the more **acidic** the water becomes. This process, called ocean acidification, threatens billion-dollar crab, lobster, oyster, and clam fisheries by weakening and deforming the shells.

Salmon are often poisoned by **herbicides**, **pesticides**, and other chemicals that drain into bays. Also the small bits of metal that come off of cars when brakes are applied wash into rivers. The metal is toxic to salmon; it harms their ability to find their way back to their home stream to breed.

Scientists are very concerned with ocean acidification in the northern Pacific and Bering Sea, because these places contain some of the most valuable and healthy fisheries in the world.

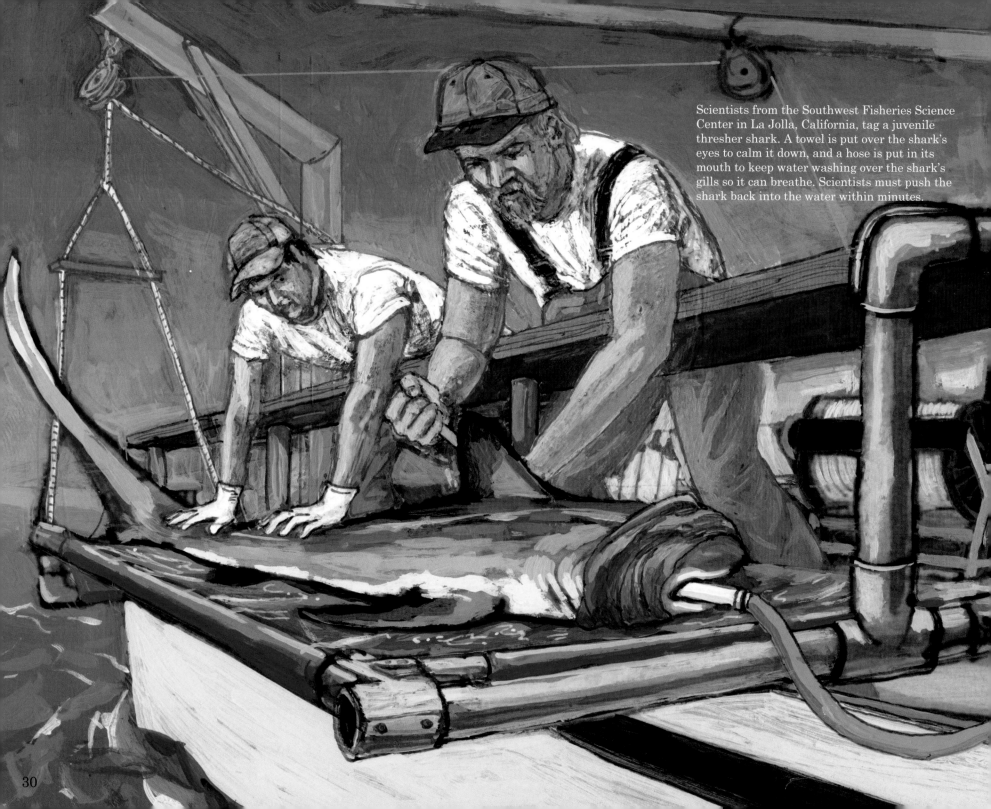

Scientists from the Southwest Fisheries Science Center in La Jolla, California, tag a juvenile thresher shark. A towel is put over the shark's eyes to calm it down, and a hose is put in its mouth to keep water washing over the shark's gills so it can breathe. Scientists must push the shark back into the water within minutes.

Tracking Fish

NOAA scientists attach tags to fish to get a better understanding of where their habitats are, their migration patterns, and how many are caught from fishing activities. Some tags, including **passive integrated transponder (PIT) tags** and acoustic tags, identify individual fish with codes like social security numbers. PIT tags are the size of rice grains and are injected into fish; acoustic tags are as big as corn kernels and are sewn into fish. After the fish are released back into the water, sensors pick up electrical signals from PIT tags or sounds emitted from acoustic tags.

Other types of tags, such as **archival tags**, record the swimming depth, water temperature, body temperature, and location of a fish anywhere on Earth for up to four years. The cylindrical three-inch-long tags are sewn into the gut of a fish. Scientists follow the movements of black sea bass for thousands of miles from New Jersey to Canada, and albacore tuna are tracked all the way from the U.S. West Coast to Japan. Sometimes, in Hawaii, the tag on a big sunfish suddenly records very low light and warm temperature, which mean a shark has eaten the fish!

Off the Southern California coast, NOAA scientists and longline fishermen tag thresher sharks by catching and releasing them. The thick white longline rips through the water reeling in hundreds of hooks baited with sardines. Occasionally, a thresher shark is pulled up fighting against the line. Some of them are so strong that they straighten the thick steel hooks in their fight to escape. Once a shark is in the tagging cradle, a thin plastic spaghetti tag is inserted near its dorsal fin. A fisherman who recaptures the shark can call the phone number on the yellow tag to report the recovery. Thresher sharks use their long powerful tails like bullwhips to stun or kill their prey. Once a thresher smacked a scientist in the head with its tail and knocked him out.

Further north in eastern Washington State, millions of juvenile salmon are caught in pipes and funneled to a salmon-tagging facility on the Snake River. The taggers inject PIT tags into endangered chinooks and steelheads. During the busy spring salmon runs, between 5,000 and 20,000 PIT tags are injected every day. A lot of fish have to be tagged because only 1 in 1,000 returns alive to the river.

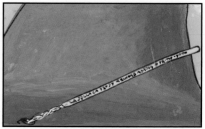

A spaghetti tag being punched into a thresher shark

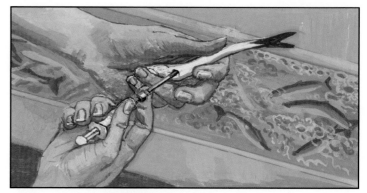

A tagger injects a PIT tag into a juvenile salmon.

A bright green spaghetti tag on this albacore tuna indicates that it has an archival tag in its abdomen.

A fisherman reels in a black sea bass with a numbered red spaghetti tag.

Tidal Wetlands

Scientists also tag shrimp and other crustaceans to gain a better understanding of how they interact with their habitats. Most fish and shellfish caught in commercial and recreational fisheries grew up along the coastline. Salt marshes and sea grass beds provide food and shelter for young fish, crabs, and shrimp. When the fish and crustaceans mature, they swim out into the ocean. Salt marshes are low-lying areas in bays where the water rises and falls with the tides. The water in salt marshes varies in salinity as the ocean water enters on a flood tide and freshwater flows out on an ebb tide. Sea grass beds consist of flowering plants growing in the sediment of the seafloor. The plants prevent erosion and protect marine animals from strong currents and wave action.

Across the United States, rising sea levels, increased wave erosion, and human develoment are drowning these habitats. In many parts of the nation, developers want to build housing, malls, and marinas on wetlands, but conservationists don't want the areas touched at all. To handle their opposing views, NOAA scientists need to know the extent to which fish and shrimp depend on the salt marshes and sea grass beds.

Mud-covered researchers collect samples from different areas in marshes to learn what shrimp need to survive. Marsh habitat is restored or created by using a variety of earth-moving equipment and by planting native marsh grasses.

Shrimp cannot be tagged on the surface of their bodies because they frequently shed their exoskeletons. Scientists inject colored paint to get permanent marks into the underlying muscle. Now they can identify individuals. Next the shrimp are released inside nets in different places in the marsh. When the shrimp are recovered, scientists can see how much each one grew in each location.

This barrier, called a **sand sock**, protects a salt marsh against waves and erosion in the Gulf of Mexico. Sea trout, red drum, mullet, crabs, and shrimp grow up in this type of ecosystem.

Coral Reefs

Tidal wetlands and coral reefs provide essential nursery grounds for fish and protect shorelines from storms. It is important to protect and restore coral reefs because they are among the most productive and diverse sea-life habitats in the world. The Nassau grouper and other important food fish species find food and shelter in coral reefs. Divers want to see the brightly colored fish and millions of different species of organisms that live in and around the reefs.

Coral reefs face many threats. In the warm tropical Pacific and the Caribbean Sea, ocean acidification threatens coral reefs. The increased acidity harms their growth process. The reefs face other dangers such as grounded ships, carelessly laid anchors that smash the reefs apart, and destructive fishing practices that use poisons and explosives to stun or scare fish out of hiding. And overfishing of algae eaters like the damselfish has allowed the algae to smother coral reefs.

Autonomous underwater vehicle (AUV)

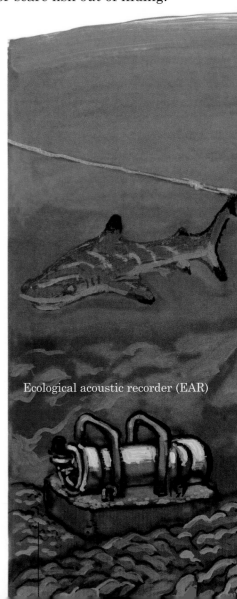

Ecological acoustic recorder (EAR)

From Guam to Puerto Rico, there are great efforts to restore coral reefs. Experiments are under way to regrow coral reefs in the Caribbean. Scientists are attempting to see how well coral larvae will settle and grow on cement and ceramic structures. Also swimming robots called autonomous underwater vehicles (AUVs) make extremely detailed maps to assess the health of the reefs.

In Hawaii, scientists are listening to coral reefs with ecological acoustic recorders (EARs). These subaquatic devices recognize sound patterns such as spawning shrimp that pop like crispy rice cereal and other patterns called coral bleaching events that indicate when coral dies. NOAA is working to keep reefs healthy to support fish populations and tourism.

Artificial coral reef

Deep-Water Habitats

In waters thousands of feet deeper than coral reefs, live rockfish, cod, snapper, and other bottom-dwelling fish. These fish are popular food items—they're tasty and full of protein—so they sustain multibillion-dollar fisheries.

Many of these fish have special adaptations to hunt. Huge eyes allow them to see in the minimal light. Some can change their skin color to blend into sand, pebbles, or mud for better camouflage.

Tagging bottom-dwelling fish and using **sonar** give scientists a better idea of how these fish live in their habitats. NOAA survey ships tow torpedo-shaped scanners that emit and receive high-frequency sound waves. It takes a long time to survey large areas of the seabed. NOAA ship crews call it "mowing the lawn," as they steer the ship back and forth scanning the ocean floor. The sound technology is so advanced that it can produce clear images of seabed habitats and even individual animals like sharks and squid.

A side-scan sonar being towed by a survey ship

A remotely operated vehicle descends into the deep on a cable that sends pictures up to the ship.

Scientists also use special cameras and robots to film and photograph the fish. All of this equipment helps scientists count the fish, measure their size, and map where they live.

Even though bottom-dwelling fish are hard to reach, many of them have been overfished because fishing gear can extend to these great depths. Sometimes fishing is prohibited in places called Marine Protected Areas. It is far easier for slow-growing and maturing fish, like rockfish and red snapper, to regenerate their numbers when fishing pressure is reduced. Marine mammals and fish that are too young to be caught need protection from fishing gear used on the ocean floor. **Bycatch** is the word used to describe the living creatures that are unintentionally caught by fishing gear.

A loggerhead sea turtle enters a shrimp trawl.

Bycatch

Shrimp fishermen in the Gulf of Mexico sometimes catch weird things in their nets: microwave ovens, World War II shell casings, gold coins from the 1700s, and hundreds of golf balls hit off of cruise ships, to name a few. Sea turtles and juvenile red snappers are also accidentally caught in shrimp trawls. NOAA regulations protect animals such as red snappers because they were nearly wiped out after years of unregulated fishing. These regulations and federal laws like the Endangered Species Act also protect sea turtles whose numbers have been reduced to dangerously low levels by accidental capture, pollution, and habitat loss. Researchers in a lab in Pascagoula, Mississippi, have developed devices called turtle excluder devices that can be installed in shrimp nets so juvenile fish and turtles can escape.

When a turtle swims into a shrimp net, it bumps into a turtle excluder device. The turtle can swim out of a flap before getting caught in the back of the net.

Around the country, fishermen and scientists have worked together for years to improve fishing gear and techniques so they only catch the target animals. In the eastern tropical Pacific, dolphins often swim above schools of yellowfin tuna. So in the late 1970s and early 1980s, U.S. tuna boats would locate schools of tuna by looking for dolphins on the surface. Boats corralled both the tuna and the dolphins into large purse seines. Nearly half a million dolphins died each year in the nets. Dolphins are mammals and breathe air like humans, so when they were trapped underwater in the nets, they drowned. Fishing boat captains and biologists developed a technique to save them called "backing down." The captain reverses the boat to curve the purse seine and to make the back end of the net sink underwater so the trapped dolphins can swim away. In extreme cases, scientists and fishermen have been known to risk their lives diving into nets to help the dolphins.

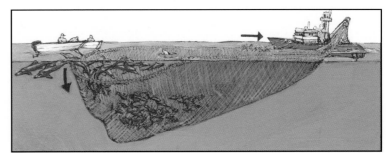

A large purse seiner backs down while dolphins escape out of the end of the net. The dolphins swim higher in the net than the tuna.

A disentanglement response team uses a saw on a long pole to free a North Atlantic right whale caught in fishing lines.

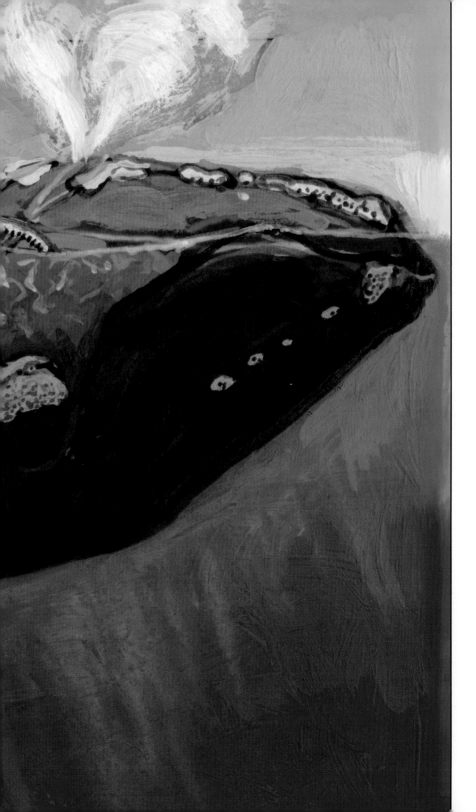

Protecting Marine Mammals

Protecting marine animals often creates conflicts between the needs of animals and people. Fishing grounds are also habitats and migratory routes of marine mammals. On the East Coast, fishing gear sometimes entangles North Atlantic right whales. Disentanglement response teams, who receive a permit from the NOAA Fisheries Service, cut the lines when they can reach the animals. Only a fraction of the whales are disentangled. Right whales are extremely endangered: Only about 300 to 400 of them exist in the wild. And a warning system off the coast near Boston, Massachusetts, alerts freighters to reduce speed if whales are nearby, so the huge ships don't collide with them.

Fishermen in Alaska trawling for pollock must stay away from threatened Steller sea lion breeding grounds called rookeries to protect the food source of young sea lions learning to forage.

Hawaiian monk seals also get entangled in fishing gear. The seals are extremely endangered. There may be only 1,200 individuals alive today. Many young seals are eaten by sharks in the Northwest Hawaiian islands, or starve from lack of food. The seals use sandy beaches to rest, **molt**, **mate**, and raise their cubs. Guidelines say that people should stay at least one hundred feet away from the vulnerable seals. Often hotel owners and surfers complain because areas of the beach have to be closed off. Biologists and volunteer groups guard the seals and try to explain the situation to upset people.

Hawaiian monk seals wiggle up the beach to shed their old fur or molt.

Stock Assessments

Scientists collect and analyze enormous amounts of information from a variety of sources to set catch limits on fish and shellfish. The more tags they receive from fishermen, the better they can keep track of fish populations. NOAA acoustic surveys and fish catches help scientists estimate the size and ages of fish populations. The records of observers and port agents contribute to the picture by showing how fishing activities affect the food web.

Information about marine life is only part of the puzzle. NOAA also monitors the number of fishing boats on the water and fishing-gear improvements because each improvement makes overfishing a bigger threat. Sociologists and economists interview fishermen and their families to see how catch limits are affecting them.

Stock assessments, the culmination of all this research, are long, detailed reports on the status of fish stocks, marine mammals, sea turtles, marine plants, marine invertebrates, and the marine ecosystems in which they live. Stock assessments help the NOAA Fisheries Service and the Fishery Management Councils decide where, when, and how much fishing can occur during each season. There are eight regional councils in the United States: New England, Mid-Atlantic, South Atlantic, Gulf of Mexico, Caribbean, Pacific, North Pacific, and Western Pacific. Each region is responsible for a 200-nautical-mile territory extending off of its coasts called the Exclusive Economic Zone (EEZ).

Enforcement

In 1976, the U.S. government created the Exclusive Economic Zone (EEZ) to stop fishing vessels from other countries from overfishing off of the coasts of the United States and its U.S. territories. Now only fishing vessels from the United States can fish inside of the 200-nautical-mile border. The NOAA Fisheries Service implements regulations to stop overfishing, reduce bycatch, and protect habitats. Fishing on the open ocean used to be a lawless free-for-all like the Wild West: Whoever caught the most fish the fastest won. Today NOAA's Office of Law Enforcement and the U.S. Coast Guard try to prevent illegal activities such as fishing out of season, fishing in restricted areas, and exceeding catch limits.

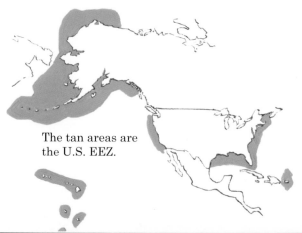

The tan areas are the U.S. EEZ.

A U.S. Coast Guard cutter prepares to board a foreign fishing boat illegally fishing inside the U.S. EEZ.

In one case, a Coast Guard cutter caught a foreign fishing vessel illegally harvesting salmon in the North Pacific Ocean. The Coast Guard waited three days to receive permission from the foreign government to board the vessel. During the delay, the fishermen threw all of the fish overboard. When the Coast Guard finally received approval to board the vessel and saw that all of the salmon had been discarded, a NOAA Fisheries Service special agent who was part of the boarding team scraped up scales he found in the empty fish hold. DNA tests revealed that the scales belonged to salmon, and the crew was charged in court.

In Gloucester, Massachusetts, an agent makes sure that the 1,500 boats on her computer screen are fishing in the right places. Every boat has a permit for scallops, whiting, or other specific catches. The boats can also be tracked by cameras and satellites.

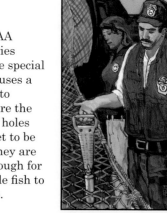

A NOAA Fisheries Service special agent uses a spade to measure the size of holes in a net to be sure they are big enough for juvenile fish to escape.

Stewardship

A NOAA biologist in New England said, "We try to gather the most accurate information possible because the regulations we make have a direct impact on people's livelihood." The NOAA Fisheries Service allows the fishing industry to catch the maximum amount of fish while leaving enough of them alive to maintain the population. Smart planning in the past ten years has cut the number of overfished species in half. Fishing for food or fun creates a lot of jobs and money, but overfishing must be stopped. Fisheries management can be complex, but there are some fairly simple things people can do to be better stewards of the ocean.

The NOAA Ship *Miller Freeman* surveys pollock at Renshaw Point in Alaska.

Homework makes most people groan, but doing a little bit on NOAA Web sites can help before buying fish at a restaurant or a store. The sites show if a species is overfished and how to tell if a fish is fresh. Pollution from lawn fertilizers, pesticides, and septic systems harms fish habitats, so ecologists encourage people to check for leaks and use chemicals sparingly. Proper disposal of trash is also important: Animals can get entangled in debris, or turtles and seabirds can mistake floating plastic trash for food. Through research, education, and enforcement, the NOAA Fisheries Service, its partners in the fishing industry, and you can ensure that future generations will enjoy what healthy marine ecosystems can provide.

Glossary

Acidic – containing acid, or acid-forming

Algae – small plants without roots or stems that grow in water or on damp surfaces

Amphipod – a type of very small crustacean, such as a sand flea

Angler – a person who uses a fishing rod to fish rather than a net

Aquaculture – the breeding, rearing, and harvesting of plants and animals in natural and human-made water enviroments, including ponds, rivers, lakes, and the ocean.

Archival tag – an electronic data-logging device that records the swimming depth, water temperature, body temperature, and location of a fish. The data are stored for up to four years.

Bait – a small amount of food used to attract a fish or animal so you can catch it

Body harness – a set of straps and metal pieces that connect a fisherman to a chair on a ship or boat

Buoy – a floating marker in the ocean or in a river

Bycatch – the living creatures that are unintentionally captured by fishing gear

Catch limit – a weight limit on fish that fishermen can catch in a fishing season

Copepod – a type of very small marine crustacean, such as an ostracod

Corral – to gather together a group of animals or things in an enclosed area

Crustacean – a sea creature that has an outer skeleton, such as a crab, lobster, or shrimp

Echo sounder – a device that uses sound waves to calculate the depth of a body of water or the location of underwater objects

Ecosystem – a community of animals and plants interacting with the land, water, weather, and the surrounding human activities

Estuary – a place where rivers and streams flow into the ocean and freshwater mixes with seawater

Euphausiid – the scientific name for many species of tiny crustaceans also known as krill

Fertilize – to begin production in an egg by causing sperm to join with the egg; to add a substance such as manure or chemicals to soil to make it richer so that crops grow better

Fillet – to remove the bones from (a fish)

Fish stock – a part of a fish population usually with a particular migration pattern, specific spawning grounds, and subject to a distinct fishery

Fishery – the occupation of fishing and a place where fish are caught in the wild or a place where fish are grown commercially

Fishing season – the weeks or months during which it is legal to catch a kind of fish

Gill net – a flat mesh net anchored to the ocean floor and held upright by buoys. Holes in the net catch the target fish by entangling its gills.

Gyre – a giant circular oceanic current

Hatchery – a place for hatching eggs, especially poultry or fish

Herbicides – chemicals used to destroy or inhibit plant growth

Hold – the part of the ship where cargo, such as fish, is stored

Hull – the frame or body of a boat or ship

Keel – a long beam along the bottom of a boat or ship that holds it together

Longline – a type of deep-sea fishing gear consisting of a long main line anchored to the ocean floor to which shorter lines with baited hooks are fastened at intervals

Mate – to join together for reproduction

Molt – when the outer covering of fur, feathers, or skin comes off a bird or an animal so that a new covering can grow

Nutrients – something that is needed by people, animals, and plants to stay strong and healthy. Proteins, minerals, and vitamins are all nutrients.

Otoliths – ear bones of a fish

Pelagic – of or relating to the open sea; living in the upper layers of the open sea

Pesticides – chemicals used to kill pests, such as insects

Phytoplankton – tiny plants that float or drift in oceans, rivers, or lakes

PIT tag – a microchip the size of a grain of rice that is injected into a fish. When scanned, it will give an individual ten-digit number.

Pots – traps in the form of cages or baskets designed to catch fish or crustaceans

Predator – an animal that lives by hunting other animals for food. Killer whales, seals, and sharks are predators.

Prey – an animal that is hunted by another animal for food

Purse seine – a net surrounds a school of fish and then is drawn closed

Runoff – the flow of water from rain, melting snow, or other sources, over land

Fish Names and Geographic Ranges

Sand sock – a soil-filled cloth barrier meant to protect an area from flood or build up an area for erosion control

Sonar – an instrument used to calculate the depth of water or the location of underwater objects

Spawning – the release of eggs to be fertilized

Species – one of the groups into which animals or plants are divided according to their shared characteristics

Stock assessment – the biological and statistical information used to assess and specify the present and probable future conditions of a fish, crustacean, or marine mammal population

Thermocline – a region below the surface layer of the sea or lake, where the temperature decreases rapidly with increasing depth

Trawl – a large net shaped like a bag

Upwelling – a rising of seawater; when winds and Earth's rotation push surface water away, and cold nutrient-rich water from the deep ocean rises to take its place

Vertebrae – the small bones that make up the backbone

Zooplankton – tiny animals that float or drift in oceans, rivers, or lakes

Albacore tuna (*Thunnus alalunga*) – in tropical, subtropical, and temperate waters of the Atlantic, Indian, and Pacific oceans

Black rockfish (*Sebastes melanops*) – in the Pacific Ocean from Amchitka Island, Alaska, to Huntington Beach, California

Black sea bass (*Centropristis striata*) – along the U.S. Atlantic coast from the Gulf of Maine to the Gulf of Mexico

Blue marlin (*Makaira nigricans*) – in the Atlantic Ocean from New England to Uruguay; in the Caribbean Sea; in the Gulf of Mexico

Bluefin tuna (*Thunnus thynnus*) – in the western Atlantic Ocean from Newfoundland to the Gulf of Mexico; in the eastern Atlantic Ocean from Iceland to the Canary Islands and into the Mediterranean Sea

Cod (family Gadidae) – in the Atlantic Ocean from Greenland to North Carolina; in the northern Pacific Ocean from California to Japan; throughout the Bering Sea

Damselfish (family Pomacentridae) – in tropical seas worldwide

Halibut (*Hippoglossus stenolepis*) – in the coastal waters of the northeastern Pacific Ocean from California to Alaska, along the Aleutian Islands and into the Bering Sea

Mahi-mahi (*Coryphaena hippurus*) – also called dolphin fish, in tropical and subtropical seas worldwide

Mullet (*Mugil cephalus*) – also called striped mullet, in the Atlantic Ocean from Cape Cod, Massachusetts, to the Gulf of Mexico; in the Pacific Ocean from Southern California to Chile

Northern anchovy (*Engraulis mordax*) – in the Pacific Ocean from British Columbia, Canada, to Baja, Mexico; in the Gulf of California

Pollock (*Pollachius virens*) – in the Atlantic Ocean from Labrador to Cape Hatteras, North Carolina; (*Theragra chalcogramma*) throughout the northern Pacific Ocean with the most in the Bering Sea

Red drum (*Sciaenops ocellatus*) – also called redfish, in the Atlantic Ocean from the Gulf of Maine to the Gulf of Mexico; more common in warmer waters

Red snapper (*Lutjanus campechanus*) – in the Atlantic Ocean from North Carolina to the Florida Keys; in the Gulf of Mexico

Salmon (family Salmonidae) – several species, including coho, chum, pink, chinook, and Atlantic; in the northern Pacific Ocean from California to Alaska to Japan; in the Arctic Ocean; in the Atlantic Ocean from Canada to the Delaware River

Salmon shark (*Lamna ditropis*) – in the northern Pacific Ocean

Steelhead (*Oncorhynchus mykiss*) – also called rainbow trout, in freshwater from Alaska to Baja, California; in salt water from Southern California to the Bering Sea

Swordfish (family Xiphiidae) – in tropical, subtropical, and temperate seas worldwide

Thesher shark (*Alopias vulpinus*) – in the Atlantic, Indian, and Pacific oceans; in the Mediterranean Sea

Tonguefish (family Cynoglossidae) – in subtropical seas worldwide

Vermilion snapper (*Rhomboplites aurorubens*) – also called night snapper, in tropical waters from Cape Hatteras, North Carolina, to Brazil; in the Gulf of Mexico

White sea bass (*Atractoscion nobilis*) – in the Pacific Ocean from Juneau, Alaska, to Baja, California

Whiting (*Merluccius bilinearis*) – also called silver hake, in the Atlantic Ocean from Newfoundland to South Carolina

Yellowfin tuna (*Thunnus albacares*) – throughout the Pacific Ocean, most abundant in between Baja, California, Hawaii, and Japan; in tropical and subtropical waters of the Atlantic Ocean

Yellowtail (genus *Seriola*) – also called yellowtail jack, in the Pacific Ocean from British Columbia to Chile

Index